Assurance

Twenty Tests for
God's Children

Selected Scriptures from 1 John

SUSAN HECK

Assurance
Twenty Test for God's Children
By Susan J. Heck

Cover design by Melanie Schmidt

ISBN 978-1-936141-10-4

Printed in the United States of America

To my seven grandchildren:
Jackson, Judah, Ember, Isaiah
Josiah, Brooklyn and Ethan,
whom I pray with all my heart
will one day be "little children" of God.

Introduction

As you and I walk on our journey here on planet earth, we face many uncertainties. There are the uncertainties of war in various places, and we wonder how these wars will affect us in the future. Will they attack American soil? Are we in the end times? Many people feel uncertain about their financial future. Recently, many have lost retirement savings and investments in the stock market. Large numbers of Americans are out of work and having difficulty finding employment. So we might ask, "What about my future? Do I have enough to live on if the Lord tarries?"

There are also many uncertainties about family relationships. "Will my spouse die before I do?" "Will someone I love get some dreadful disease?" For those of you who are single, you might be wondering, "Will I ever get married?" For those of you who are childless, you might be asking, "Will I ever have children?" These and many more questions come to our minds when we think about our future and what it holds, and these uncertainties cannot be answered, at least by mortal man.

However, for the believer in Jesus Christ, there are *things we can be certain about*; there are things we don't have to wonder about. We can be certain about the character of God, for example. He is holy, just, righteous, all-powerful, all-knowing and good. We can also be certain He will come again to judge the living and the dead. And we can be certain that some will leave this life and enter into eternity with Him, and some will not. You might be asking, "How do I know if I will be among those who will enter into the Kingdom with Him on that day?" John answers that question in 1 John 5:13, "These things I have written to you who believe in the name of the Son of God, that you may know that you have eternal life, and that you may continue to believe in the name of the Son of God." You do not have to be uncertain as to where you will spend eternity. John comes to the end of his letter and says, "Look, all the things I have written in this epistle, I have written to you who believe Jesus is God, and I have written this letter that you might know for certain you have eternal life." The word *know* that is used here is not "I hope so." It does not even mean you have a growing assurance of your salvation. Instead, it is a word that indicates this is an absolute assurance—you can know for sure that you have eternal life. You do not need to doubt. How can one know they have eternal life? By the valid tests John has given—by self-examination, as Paul would say in 2 Corinthians 13:5, "Examine yourselves as to whether you are in the faith. Test yourselves. Do you not know yourselves, that Jesus Christ is in you?—unless indeed you are disqualified."

Now you might ask the question, "If John is writing to believers, then why do they have to examine themselves? Wouldn't those reading this epistle be believers?" John would hope so, just as I would hope that all of you who are reading this booklet are believers. You might think that because you attend church regularly or attend Bible studies that you know God. But these things do not determine that one knows God. In fact, we should not presume that those who read the Word or even study the Word know the Author of the Word. Scripture is filled with examples of those who did those things, and we have recorded in Scripture where Jesus calls them blind leaders of the blind, hypocrites and fools (Matthew 23). Our Christianity is never based on reading or studying the Word, or even praying, but it is revealed by an ongoing examination of our life.

In this booklet we are going to look at a series of 20 valid proofs from 1 John that will help you examine your own personal life and evaluate whether or not you have eternal life. I trust that these 20 tests will give you a confident assurance that you know Him. If not, I pray you will make that commitment to follow Him wholeheartedly.

Chapter 1

1. The test of having partnership or fellowship with Christ and the Father.

> That which we have seen and heard we declare to you, that you also may have fellowship with us; and truly our fellowship is with the Father and with His Son Jesus Christ (1 John 1:3).

John says we can have a living relationship with the living God. Think what it means to have *fellowship with Christ and the Father*! The word means partnership. In secular Greek the word meant to have common ownership, like property that a married couple would jointly own together. American Christians often say, "Let's get together and have fellowship," and what we mean is let's get together and have coffee and donuts. That is not fellowship in the biblical sense. Fellowship means we share something in common. That commonality is our union with Christ. If we do not have a personal relationship with Him, accepting the facts of his incarnation, death, burial and resurrection, we have no fellowship with one another, and we have no fellowship, no partnership, with Him. It is only possible to have this fellowship with the Father through his Son Jesus Christ. As 1 John 5:11 states, "And this is the testimony: that God has given us eternal life, and this life is in His Son." In contrast to what some believe, Jesus says in John 14:6 that "No one comes to the Father except through me." By the way, the Greek tense here in 1 John 1:3 is to keep on having fellowship. That certainly is a comfort to the believer, as no man can pluck us out of the Father's hand. It is a forever deal! Would you say you have embraced Christ on His terms and that you now have fellowship with Him? If you can answer yes to that question, then this is evidence that you are born of God. Now this fellowship with Christ, this partnership that you and I have, has some wonderful benefits. One of those benefits is joy. And not just plain old joy, but fullness of joy, which brings us to test number two.

2. The test of joy.

> And these things we write to you that your joy may be full (1 John 1:4).

John is saying that one of his purposes for writing this book is that those who read it will have fullness of joy. The fact that you and I have partnership with the living God and have life eternal should bring us joy as nothing in this life can. *Joy* is cheerfulness or calm delight. I like that definition—calm delight—don't you? The word *full* means to cover over or to be complete. Would you say that your life exhibits joy that is complete? If not, that might be a valid indication that you are not redeemed or that there is some sin in your life. There should be no such thing as a gloomy Christian. Christians should have joy and they should have fullness of joy! If you do not have joy in your life, then maybe you need to look carefully at test number three, which validates whether one is born of God or not.

3. The test of confessing our sins.

> If we confess our sins, He is faithful and just to forgive us our sins and to cleanse us from all unrighteousness (1 John 1:9).

Another valid test that you are born of God is that you are in the habit of confessing your sins. Genuine believers confess their sins. John tells us in the next verse that those who are not born of God claim they have no sin: "If we say that we have not sinned, we make Him a liar, and His word is not in us" (1 John 1:10). What does it mean to *confess our sins*? It means you are a person who is conscious of a wrong-doing and are convicted that it is sin, and you admit it. For example, "Lord, I know that my temper today with my child or my husband was sin, as your Word says I am to put away all anger." "Lord, I know that my jealousy over this friend is sin, as your Word says love is not jealous." "Lord, I know that today my frustration with people, interruptions, or circumstances has been sinful, but your Word says all things work together for my good, so I know that you allowed even these interruptions." When we are walking in the light we will be conscious of those things. We will not try to excuse our sin away, but we will admit it, confess it, and endeavor to forsake it. The Greek tense for *confess* is to keep on confessing. Believers in Jesus Christ are always in the habit of confessing their sins. If this describes you, then you can be confident of your salvation.

4. The test of a broken pattern of sinning.

> Whoever abides in Him does not sin. Whoever sins has neither seen Him nor known Him (1 John 3:6). See also 1 John 2:1; 3:4-6; 3:8, 9; 5:18.

John says that those who abide in God do not sin! You might be asking, "How can this be?" "How can a Christian not sin?" Some have taken this to mean that Christians never sin. They call it the doctrine of perfection. I have met a lot of Christians, and I must say I have never met one who does not sin. If you find one, let me know. I would like to meet them, and of course, I would like to ask their spouse or their children or their closest friends if they sin. Christians sin. Even Paul admits his battle with his sinful flesh in Romans 7. He explains the wrestling that goes on within himself, that he wants to do what is right but he ends up doing what is not right (Romans 7:19). He ends his discourse by saying, "O wretched man that I am! Who will deliver me from this body of death?" (Romans 7:24). Paul sinned. Moses, who was the meekest man on earth, sinned. He got angry! And the result was that he did not get to enter the Promised Land. Also, David, who was a man after God's own heart, sinned. He sinned grossly by committing adultery with Bathsheba and then having her husband murdered to try to cover it up! The result of his sin was the death of his child when it was only 7 days old, plus a myriad of other disastrous results!

So what is John saying when he states that those who abide in Him do not sin? John is talking about a habit of sin, just as mentioned in verse 4: "Whoever commits sin also commits lawlessness, and sin is lawlessness" (1 John 3:4). A person who claims to be a Christian, and yet has an ongoing pattern of sin in their life, proves to be a spurious Christian, one who does not have a regenerated heart. If there is no change, no growing toward Christ's likeness, and no change of lifestyle, then John makes it clear in 1 John 3:8 that "He who sins is of the devil, for the devil has sinned from the beginning. For this purpose the Son of God was manifested, that He might destroy the works of the devil." One man put it well. "The believer may fall into sin but he will not walk in it."[1] Or as the early church father, Chrysostom, said "To sin is human; but to persevere in sin is not human but altogether satanic."

---

[1] Donald Burdick, *The Letters of John the Apostle* (Chicago, IL: Moody Press, 1985) p. 239.

John goes on to say, "Whoever sins has neither seen Him nor known Him" (1 John 3:6b). Those who practice sin not only cannot *see Him*—they are spiritually blind—but also do not know Him. What does it mean to *know Him*? It means to come to know. If you continue in sin, then John says you have not come to know him. John is talking about a knowledge that is spiritual as well as experiential. How could we know Him and live in habitual sin? The writer to the Hebrews would give us a fearful warning if we held to that view: "For if we sin willfully after we have received the knowledge of the truth, there no longer remains a sacrifice for sins, but a certain fearful expectation of judgment, and fiery indignation which will devour the adversaries" (Hebrews 10:26-27). We cannot live in ongoing sin and claim that we know God. This really goes with test number 5.

5. The test of obedience.

> Now by this we know that we know Him, if we keep His commandments. He who says, 'I know Him,' and does not keep His commandments, is a liar, and the truth is not in him. But whoever keeps His word, truly the love of God is perfected in him. By this we know that we are in Him (1 John 2:3-5). See also 1 John 3:22-24 and 5:2, 3.

Did you notice John did not say, "By this we know that we know Him, if we walked down the aisle at a revival"? He did not say, "By this we know that we know him, if we said a prayer to ask Jesus to come into our heart." There is a valid test to make certain one is a believer in Christ, and it has nothing to do with the past, but it has everything to do with the present. It has to do with keeping His commandments.

John says we can know—we can be sure—we are a child of the King. How can I know for sure I am a Christian? John says—here it is—the answer you have been waiting for. You can be sure you know Him *if* you keep His commandments. I can know facts about Christ and yet not know Him personally in the sense of what John is saying here. For example, I may say to you, I know the President of the United States. What I mean is I know facts about him. Facts like: he is the president; and I know the names of his wife and children. I know other facts about him because I read the newspaper or watch the news on television. But do I know him? Do I have a personal relationship with Him? No, I do not, as I've never even met him. We must be so careful in assuming that we are believers because we say we know Christ. We may read about Him in the Word, and hear about Him at church or from the lips of others, but does that equate with a personal relationship with Him? No!

So John says you can know for sure that you know Him, if you keep His commandments. What does it mean to keep his commandments? The word *keep* here has the idea of a spirit of obedience. It means to guard and keep safe as a precious thing. By the way, this is not because we have to, but because we want to. As John said in 1 John 5:3, "For this is the love of God, that we keep His commandments. And His commandments are not burdensome." God's commands should be a delight and not a burden. They are not weighty or heavy. Obeying God should not be a heavy duty; but it should be a joyful duty, and there should be a freedom in our obedience. Sin is heavy and burdensome, but not obedience.

For example, I know people who claim to know Christ and yet they will not follow the Lord in baptism. They don't think it is necessary, or they are uncomfortable getting up in front of people, so they disregard God's commandment to be baptized. It is a burden to them. Or another person will say, "I am a Christian, but I don't need to go to church. I can worship God here at home." They neglect to obey Hebrews 10:25, which is a command: "Not forsaking the assembling of ourselves together, as is the manner of some, but exhorting one another, and so much the more as you see the Day approaching." It is a burden for them to get up, get the kids dressed, and go to church. That type of thinking is foreign to New Testament Christianity. It should be a joy and delight to obey the Lord. We do not have the option of only keeping the commandments that we find convenient.

The Christian life is not a spiritual smorgasbord where I can pick and choose what I want to obey or not obey. I once heard of a man who was so disturbed about the fact that His fellowship with God was not right, that he stayed up reading the Word of God until he found which commandment he was disobeying. Are you that serious about obeying the Word of God? What did Jesus say in Luke 6:46? "But why do you call me 'Lord, Lord,' and do not do the things which I say?" Jesus knew that a claim to His Lordship without obeying His Lordship was no Lordship! John finishes his thought by saying, "He who says, 'I know Him,' and does not keep His commandments, is a liar, and the truth is not in him. But whoever keeps His word, truly the love of God is perfected in him. By this we know that we are in Him" (1 John 2:4, 5). John goes on to say in verse 6 that our talk must match our walk. And this is our sixth self-examination test.

6. The test of walking as Christ walked.

> He who says he abides in Him ought himself also to walk just as He walked (1 John 2:6).

John says that those who claim they abide in God must walk as He walked. The word *ought* expresses a special personal obligation. For example, if I borrow money from you, I ought to pay it back. It is my moral obligation to you. John is saying you owe this to God after all He has done for you. He has sent His son to be the propitiation for your sins. His Son died for your sins and therefore it is your moral obligation to walk as He walked. What does it mean to *walk*? It means to walk in an orderly manner following a prescribed pattern. So we might say walking means to follow a pattern or a rule. I remember when I was a child in school we would play the game, "Follow the Leader." If you remember that game one person would lead a group of children and everyone had to follow exactly where the leader walked and do exactly what the leader did. That is the idea in what John is saying here. We follow His footsteps and we walk the way He walked. Walking would also indicate progress. When you walk, you don't just stand still in one place, you move forward and you move on. So it would indicate that we are growing as we walk with God, and we are making progress. John then gives another test, and this one he mentions numerous times in his little epistle, so it must be an important one.

7. The test of loving the brethren.

> He who says he is in the light, and hates his brother, is in darkness until now. He who loves his brother abides in the light, and there

> is no cause for stumbling in him. But he who hates his brother is in darkness and walks in darkness, and does not know where he is going, because the darkness has blinded his eyes (1 John 2: 9-11). See also 1 John 3:10-18; 3:23; 4:7-12; 4:20-5:2.

John says if you claim you are in the light, if you claim you are a Christian, and yet hate your brother, you are in darkness even until now. What does it mean to *hate* my brother? The word means to detest or abhor. The present tense indicates a continuous attitude of hatred rather than a momentary hatred. John himself had not been perfect in this commandment. Remember Luke 9:51-56? John and James wanted to call fire down from heaven and blast a Samaritan village out of existence because they would not let Christ come into their village. Jesus told James and John that they did not know what manner of spirit they were. The Son of Man did not come to destroy men's lives but to save them. We all have times when we forget what manner of spirit we are and that we are sons and daughters of the King. But our lives should be marked by loving others. John says if you hate your brother you are in darkness even until now. That means you are in darkness up until this moment. The person who has an ongoing attitude of hatred towards others is in darkness right up to this moment, and he has never been in any other condition but darkness. In fact, John has some pretty strong words in 1 John 3:15, where he says, "Whoever hates his brother is a murderer, and you know that no murderer has eternal life abiding in him." John makes it pretty clear that hatred in your heart is the same as murder.

In contrast to those who hate their brother, we have those who love their brother in verse 10: "He who loves his brother abides in the light, and there is no cause for stumbling in him." Now, to love our brother does not mean that we have to have some warm fuzzy affection for all believers. But it does mean that our attitude toward believers will be one of looking out for their interests above our own. We will not ignore them or despise them. That is agape love, which John is referring to here. The love that God commands is not a feeling about another person, but it is a choice we make about another person. John uses the present tense for love, just as he did for hate. In other words, it is not a sporadic moment of love, but an ongoing reality of loving the brethren. We don't say or think, "I will show an act of love today," and then don't do any other acts of love for a month. It is ongoing, as we are always looking for ways to love the brethren. Let's move on to yet another test that John gives.

8. The test of overcoming the wicked one.

> I write to you, fathers, because you have known Him who is from the beginning. I write to you, young men, because you have overcome the wicked one. I write to you, little children, because you have known the Father. I have written to you, fathers, because you have known Him who is from the beginning. I have written to you, young men, because you are strong, and the word of God abides in you, and you have overcome the wicked one (1 John 2:13-14). See also 1 John 5:4, 18.

Perhaps you are wondering who the young men are to whom John is speaking. Physically speaking, a young man in biblical times would be between the ages of 24-40. He was not a child, but he also was not an aged father either.

Spiritually speaking, young men would be men who were well-grounded in the truth, men who had been thoroughly exercised in the Christian warfare; men who were no longer weighed down by doubts and fears, but had arrived at the abiding testimony of the Spirit of God in their consciences.

Young men can discern between good and evil, and usually have a pretty good grasp on the doctrines of the faith. John says these young men in the faith have overcome the wicked one, Satan. This means they have subdued him or gotten the victory over him. The tense is a permanent victory after conflict. This does not mean that the wicked one never tempts him, but young men know what they believe and they have the Word of God grounded in their hearts and minds and Satan does not have the advantage over them. They are more aware and less vulnerable to his tactics than the babies in Christ. This is one of the ways we know that we know Christ. John will say later on in his epistle, in 1 John 5:4, "For whatever is born of God overcomes the world. And this is the victory that has overcome the world—our faith." Genuine believers overcome the world and the wicked one who controls it. Also, 1 John 5:18 says, "We know that whoever is born of God does not sin; but he who has been born of God keeps himself, and the wicked one does not touch him." The wicked one cannot touch those who are of God. When I think of the enemy I think of the prince of this world (John 12:31), which brings us to test number 9.

9. The test of not loving the world.

> Do not love the world or the things in the world. If anyone loves the world, the love of the Father is not in him. For all that is in the world—the lust of the flesh, the lust of

> the eyes, and the pride of life—is not of the Father but is of the world. And the world is passing away, and the lust of it; but he who does the will of God abides forever (1John 2:15-17). See also 1 John 4:4, 5.

Love here is agape, and it is used in a moral sense. It is a love that is supreme and a love that is due God. The word for *world* describes the world system, which opposes and is hostile toward God. So loving the world would include loving anything that is in opposition to God. It would include thoughts that are opposed to God, habits that are opposed to God, actions that are opposed to God and even relationships that are opposed to God. You don't have to be around people in the world very long before you realize what those principles and desires and values are. People living in the world think and act in a way that is very contrary to the Word of God. The Greek tense that John uses here is the present active imperative, which means to stop loving the world. *Love* is also in the present tense, which means we are not to be in constant love with the world. It is an absolute denial. God forbid that we should be in love with the world. Why would we love the world when we consider what John says in 1 John 5:19: "We know that we are of God, and the whole world lies under the sway of the wicked one."

John goes on to say that we are also not to love the things in the world. What are the things in the world? John is not saying we are not to love what is in the world like the flowers, birds, trees, and things like that. We should admire their beauty and the Creator of them. In the next verse John describes the *things* in the world, "the lust of the flesh, the lust of the eyes, and the pride of life," which we will look at momentarily. So what happens if you and I love the world?

What happens if we have values and principles and speech and goals that are like the world? John says, "If anyone loves the world, the love of the Father is not in him." The tense here reads like this: "If anyone has a continual practice of loving the world, the love of the Father is not in him." Notice there is no exception here: if *anyone* loves the world. You can be a pastor, pastor's wife, Sunday school teacher, nursery worker, or church janitor, but if you love the world, John says the love of the Father is not in you.

Let's take a closer look at what John describes as the things in the world—the three deadly sins that every believer must avoid at all costs. "For all that is in the world—the lust of the flesh, the lust of the eyes, and the pride of life—is not of the Father but is of the world."

First of all, *the lust of the flesh*. What is the lust of the flesh? *Lust* is a longing for what is forbidden. It is those desires of our flesh that want immediate self-satisfaction. *Flesh* is the sensual appetite. This would be any craving that one desires in order to satisfy their physical desires. In Galatians 5:17-21, Paul gives a pretty complete list of the lust of the flesh.

> For the flesh lusts against the Spirit and the Spirit against the flesh; and these are contrary to one another, so that you do not do the things that you wish. But if you are led by the Spirit, you are not under the law. Now the works of the flesh are evident, which are: adultery, fornication, uncleanness, lewdness, idolatry, sorcery, hatred, contentions, jealousies, outbursts of wrath, selfish ambitions, dissensions, heresies, envy,

> murders, drunkenness, revelries, and the like; of which I tell you beforehand, just as I also told you in time past, that those who practice such things will not inherit the kingdom of God (Galatians 5:17-21).

I would encourage you to take some time to look these words up and study what they mean. It is important to bring out that being hungry for food, having an appetite, is not sinful. God made our bodies to feel hunger and to eat. But when that appetite becomes out of control and we gorge or abuse our bodies, then we have fallen prey to the lust of the flesh. Or if you starve that appetite because you have some sinful desire to be ridiculously thin, then you have fallen prey to the lust of the flesh.

Let's take another appetite: our sexual appetite. There is nothing wrong with that, as God made our bodies to enjoy sexual relationship. Paul even says in 1 Corinthians 7:9b, "For it is better to marry than to burn with passion." But when that sexual appetite becomes out of control, to the point that we give way to sexual perversions such as fornication, homosexuality, adultery, bestiality, or when sex becomes an idol that is thought about constantly, we have fallen prey to the lust of the flesh. The readers of this epistle would understand this, as the city of Ephesus was rampant with pagan religions which glorified sex. Sex had become a perversion, and it was sinful.

Let's take the desire of having a home or a car or even furniture. There is nothing wrong with that. But if that desire becomes an idol to the point that you have to have more and more material things and your lust for them is never satisfied, then you have fallen prey to the lust of the flesh. Well, let's move on to the second deadly sin—*the lust of the eyes*.

What is the lust of the eyes? This is a seeking of the mental pleasures, whereas the other (lust of the flesh) is the physical gratification. This is a greedy craving that wants whatever it sees. Many people perhaps think they can get away with the lust of the eyes because that's where it ends, or so they think. They just lust with their eyes without indulging in outward sin. However, Jesus said something very different in Matthew 5:27-30.

> You have heard that it was said to those of old, "You shall not commit adultery." But I say to you that whoever looks at a woman to lust for her has already committed adultery with her in his heart. If your right eye causes you to sin, pluck it out and cast it from you; for it is more profitable for you that one of your members perish, than for your whole body to be cast into hell. And if your right hand causes you to sin, cut it off and cast it from you; for it is more profitable for you that one of your members perish, than for your whole body to be cast into hell (Matthew 5:27-30).

Jesus says lusting with the eyes is a sin worthy of damnation. Remember Job, who said he made a covenant with his eyes that he would not look lustfully upon a woman (Job 31:1)? In my opinion, the media has done more damage to the Christian world than any other thing I know. Television, movies, commercials, magazines, billboards, internet, and the like have been used to arouse lust to have things to the point that many people spend the bulk of their time shopping for things that they don't need and cannot afford. Also, the media has created a gross lust for sex. The internet has made porn so readily available to the point that we are seeing little children exploited and abused and even murdered. Manufacturers don't sell products, but they sure sell sex.

John goes on to mention the third deadly sin that is in the world—*the pride of life*. What is the pride of life? The pride of life is a boasting of one's own resources, or in the stability of earthly things. It is the Greek word *alazon*, which means braggert. William Barclay says this man is "the boastful braggart who tries to make himself out a far bigger man than he is." [2] He boasts about what he has done and what he will do. This is a person who thinks he is the Master of his destiny, he thinks he has all under control and is in control.

John points out that these things, these three deadly sins, *are not of the Father, but are of the world*. Can you imagine our Lord ever being involved in such heinous sins? Jesus himself was in the world, but you can read the Scriptures and you will not see Him delighting in the world, or involved in lusting of any kind or in any prideful boasting. He once said, "For even the Son of Man did not come to be served, but to serve, and to give His life a ransom for many" (Mark 10:45). When tempted with those things in the wilderness, as seen in Luke 4, He never once succumbed to them. And neither should we. If you love the world, my friend, you may not be certain of your eternal state, and probably should not be!

---

[2] William Barclay. *The Letters of John and Jude* (Philadelphia, PA: The Westminster Press, 1976) p. 58.

10. The test of persevering to the end.

> They went out from us, but they were not of us; for if they had been of us, they would have continued with us; but they went out that they might be made manifest, that none of them were of us (1 John 2:10).

Evidently some had gone out from the church that once had been present in the church. What does it mean *they went out*? The Greek phrase *went out* is speaking of a physical location. They went out from the church. This is not talking about church discipline or excommunication, as mentioned in Matthew 18, but a voluntary going out of their own free will. The Greek tense here means they left the church of Jesus Christ of their own accord. These were religious people, but not Christ's children. They had attached themselves to the church, but they themselves were not a part of the church of Jesus Christ. This is a sobering warning of apostasy. John says they physically went out from us, but listen, little children, the fact is they were never of us! If they had been of us, they would have continued with us. But they went out so that it would be made manifest that they were never of us. These guys proved by their going out that they were never in the faith. True believers in Jesus Christ do not fall away from the faith! They do not apostatize. If we persevere, and if we persevere to the end, it proves the sincerity of the commitment we have made. If we fall away, it proves the fact that we were never sincere or regenerated to begin with.

Well, we are half way, and maybe you are saying "I am in a heap of trouble." Dear Reader, your eternal soul is at stake. Please take time to examine yourself in light of these ten tests and then let us move on to the last half of the tests of valid faith.

Chapter 2

Perhaps some of you are feeling a little discouraged right now after reading and examining yourself in light of chapter one. Perhaps, after self-examination, you are encouraged that you appear to be one who is truly redeemed. No matter which category you find yourself in, let's move on to the final ten tests.

11. The test of the indwelling Holy Spirit.

> Now he who keeps His commandments abides in Him, and He in him. And by this we know that He abides in us, by the Spirit whom He has given us (1 John 3:24). See also 1 John 2:20, 27 and 4:13.

The Apostle John tells us that another way that we can know for sure that we are of God is by the Spirit He has given us. The word for *know* here means we can be sure that we abide in Him, we are staying in a given place, because of the Spirit in us. The Holy Spirit came into your life at the time of your conversion. He is the one who resides in you, empowers you, convicts you of sin and teaches you. This working of Him in your life is a sign that you are of God.

12. The test of belief.

> And this is His commandment: that we should believe on the name of His Son Jesus Christ and love one another, as He gave us commandment (1 John 3:23). See also 1 John 2:23, 4:2, 15; 5:1, 4, 5, 10, 13, 20.

If we took this test of belief only by itself, we would find many who would say, "Yes, I know the Lord." But we must remember what James says in his epistle: "You believe that there is one God. You do well. Even the demons believe—and tremble!" (James 2:19). James, also, is another New Testament writer that gives us many tests of our faith in his epistle.

The belief that John is referring to here is once and for all. It refers to one who continually believes. I don't just believe in Jesus today, and decide tomorrow I think He is a fake. The belief in Christ is a continual life-long belief, it is one that marks how I live my life and it stays with me to the end. As the writer to the Hebrews would tell us: "For we have become partakers of Christ if we hold the beginning of our confidence steadfast to the end" (Hebrews 3:14). This belief in Christ affects the very nature of who I am and it fleshes out in my love for God and others.

13. The test of abiding in Him.

> And we have known and believed the love that God has for us. God is love, and he who abides in love abides in God, and God in him (1 John 4:16). See also 1 John 2:27, 28.

This is an amazing verse, as John says this is a permanent knowledge that does not leave us. John says we know—we have a permanent knowledge of the love that God has toward us! One who believes in God knows the love God has for him. God's love is not some warm fuzzy feeling for us; but it is an agape love, which gives not what man wants but what he needs. Man needed forgiveness of sins and a Savior. And so God so loved the world that he gave His only begotten son, that whoever would believe in Him would not perish, but have everlasting life. That's how much God loves us. And because of that, those who have confessed Him as their Lord have received that love. John says whoever abides in love abides in God and God in him. That means God dwells in us along with His love, and we abide, or remain, in Him. This is a wonderful assurance that we have a living relationship with the living God! When we have that relationship with God, we will live in a certain way, which reflects that we are His sons and daughters. This leads us to test number 14—the test of holy living.

14. The test of holy living.

> If you know that He is righteous, you know that everyone who practices righteousness is born of Him (1 John 2:29). See also 1 John 3:3, 7.

John says everyone that is born of God does righteousness. What does righteous mean? It means to do right. Here is a person who always does what is right. So the logical conclusion is what? Everyone that is born of God does right! The person that does righteousness is born of Him; the person who does right has been regenerated. The tense indicates that the new birth has not only taken place but it is still effective. This person continues to practice righteousness. Even the Old Testament saints understood this, as David says in Psalm 15:1-2, "LORD, who may abide in Your tabernacle? Who may dwell in Your holy hill? *He who walks uprightly,* and *works righteousness,* and speaks the truth in his heart" (emphasis mine). David says, "Lord, who is truly religious? Who is your friend? Who can dwell with you?" Then he gives a list of 10 imperatives and two of those mention practicing righteousness. God did not save us to sit around and do nothing. Paul makes this very clear in Ephesians 2:10, "For we are His workmanship, created in Christ Jesus for good works, which God prepared beforehand that we should walk in them." Doing what is right will sometimes result in some consequences that might be difficult and this is test number 15.

15. The test of hatred from the world.

> Do not marvel, my brethren, if the world hates you (1 John 3:13).

John says *do not marvel*, cease wondering or stop wondering about this. Don't think it is so unusual that the world hates you. In fact, it would be unusual if the world loved us, wouldn't it? It would probably be an indicator that something is out of kilter with us. After all, the world and its system are opposed to God and all He stands for. Sometimes we forget this is what Christ said would happen and perhaps we should remind ourselves of it. Jesus is clear about this in John 15:18-19, "If the world hates you, you know that it hated Me before it hated you. If you were of the world, the world would love its own. Yet because you are not of the world, but I chose you out of the world, therefore the world hates you."

What does John mean when he says the world hates us? It means they detest us. John says don't be surprised at this, if the world hates you or detests you. The world hates us just as Cain hated his brother, Abel. Why? Because Cain's works were evil, but his brother's were righteous. "For this is the message that you heard from the beginning, that we should love one another, not as Cain who was of the wicked one and murdered his brother. And why did he murder him? Because his works were evil and his brother's righteous" (1 John 3: 11-12).

Unbelievers are not comfortable around us because we are salt and light and our righteous deeds expose their evil deeds, which cause them to feel guilt and shame. If you are not being hated by the world, my friend, it might be an indication that you are not redeemed, as Paul says, "Yes, and all who desire to live godly in Christ Jesus will suffer persecution" (2 Timothy 3:12). Praise be to God that not all of the Christian walk is difficult, as there are some wonderful joys that accompany our relationship with Christ, and we see that in test number 16.

16. The test of answered prayer.

> Now this is the confidence that we have in Him, that if we ask anything according to His will, He hears us. And if we know that He hears us, whatever we ask, we know that we have the petitions that we have asked of Him (1 John 5:14-15). See also 1 John 3:22.

First of all, as we think about prayer, notice that John says we have to ask. So often someone will come to me with a dilemma or problem, looking for an answer, and I will ask, "Have you prayed about this?" And they give me a look like "Well, I never thought of that!" Then usually I will challenge them to pray about their situation and perhaps even to fast and pray. This is usually a pretty good indicator of how much they want relief or help for their problem. Many people just want to complain about what they don't have, or how hard their life is, but few want to get on their knees and petition God for help.

The word *ask* means to beg or to crave. It is a word that is used to describe the attitude of one who is an inferior toward a superior. John says *if we ask anything*, and that is where too many people stop. Ask for anything—you mean ask for a million dollars and I get it? You mean ask for perfect health and I get it? You mean ask for a new home and I get it? Notice that isn't quite what John says. He says if we ask anything *according to His will* He hears us. What we ask of God must be in harmony with His will for us. It is truly amazing that the God of the Universe hears our prayers. What does it mean that He *hears us*? It means He listens attentively and favorably, and considers our requests seriously, just as a parent would consider a child's request if it was reasonable. We know that answered prayer is only for those who know God, as John 9:31 states, "Now we know that God does not hear sinners; but if anyone is a worshiper of God and does His will, He hears him." Or, as the Psalmist would say in Psalm 34:17, "The righteous cry out, and the LORD hears, and delivers them out of all their troubles." This is again an indication that one is born of God. As we move on to test number 17, we come to a test that is so needed in our age!

17. The test of overcoming false teachers.

> You are of God, little children, and have overcome them, because He who is in you is greater than he who is in the world (1 John 4:4).

Notice John's tenderness to them as he says *you are of God, little children*. How did they know they were of God? Because they *have overcome them*. The question might come to mind, "Overcome who?" John makes it clear in the previous verse that the *who* are the false prophets, the antichrists.

> Beloved, do not believe every spirit, but test the spirits, whether they are of God; because many false prophets have gone out into the world. By this you know the Spirit of God: Every spirit that confesses that Jesus Christ has come in the flesh is of God, and every spirit that does not confess that Jesus Christ has come in the flesh is not of God. And this is the spirit of the Antichrist, which you have heard was coming, and is now already in the world (1 John 4:1-3).

When John says they have overcome them, it means that they have subdued them with a calm confidence of final victory. This affirms to you and me that those who know Christ cannot be led astray by false teachers. You and I will not accept the false teacher or his or her teachings. Now you might ask, "How will I be able to discern false teachers? How will I overcome them?" John says *because He who is in you is greater than he who is in the world.* But beware, lest you begin thinking, "Well, I sure have discernment against error, but I wonder why so and so doesn't? I must be someone special or have a special gift!" No! Even though there is a gift of discernment according to 1 Corinthians 12:10, it is the Spirit that is in you that gives you that discernment. It is not of us; it is of God. And God is greater than Satan, who is behind all antichrists, all false teachers, and all false teaching!

Test number 18 is especially dear to my heart, and it is the one the Lord used to affirm my salvation when I finally was genuinely saved.

18. The test of no fear in judgment.

> Love has been perfected among us in this: that we may have boldness in the day of judgment; because as He is, so are we in this world. There is no fear in love; but perfect love casts out fear, because fear involves torment. But he who fears has not been made perfect in love (1 John 4: 17-18). See also 1 John 2:28.

The idea behind what John is saying is that those who are born of God have a love that is complete and therefore they have no fear of judgment to come, because they live as He lived. What does it mean to *have boldness* in the day of judgment? This word entails boldness in speaking. In fact, it was a word that described the martyrs in the early church as they faced their killers; they had confidence. It was also used to describe the free citizens of Athens who were allowed to freely speak their mind with boldness in the assembly.

John goes on to say that it is impossible for fear and love to coexist together: "There is no fear in love; but perfect love casts out fear, because fear involves torment." There is no fear in love. Fear is alarm or fright. It comes from the Greek word *phobos*, from which we get our word phobia. In fact, the Greeks had a god who was called Phobos, who was said to be dreaded because of the terror he inspired. A believer does not have that dread or fear. Fear is the dread experienced by a slave or a criminal. True love has no fear, as it is not concerned about self-preservation but surrenders to the one who is loved. The man or woman who loves God and whom God loves has no fear. They don't dread the judgment to come. They know they will be able to stand bold in the day of judgment because of the shed blood of Christ. They have been justified and have assurance of that. Before the Lord saved me I was terrified and got sick to my stomach every time the subject of the rapture was brought up. Why? Because I had not been justified and had no assurance of that, even though I thought I was a believer. This is a test of assurance, that a child of God will have boldness in the day of judgment. There will be no fear. If you are fearful, then you cannot love. What John is saying is that those who fear that coming day have not been made perfect in their love for God: "but he who fears has not been made perfect in love." A person who has a continual fear of the coming judgment is one in whom the Spirit does not reside, as he or she would by the Spirit of God have a love that has been made complete or perfect. It is the unbeliever that has a terror of the judgment to come, and they should. But one who is walking with the Lord should not have that continual fear of judgment to come.

Now I do want to stop and say that there may be times that you do have some fears about the judgment to come, and this could be due to unconfessed sin or relationships you need to make right, or perhaps sin you won't put off. You might also have some fear of judgment as you think about loved ones that are lost. But the overall life of a believer should be one of not fearing the judgment to come. There may be unconfessed sin or issues you need to deal with that perhaps are causing you to be fearful, but if your life is one of overall fear of the coming judgment, then perhaps you might want to examine that very carefully. If you are living as Jesus did, as John said, then fear should run out the door!

19. The test of loving God.

> If someone says, "I love God," and hates his brother, he is a liar; for he who does not love his brother whom he has seen, how can he love God whom he has not seen? And this commandment we have from Him: that he who loves God must love his brother also. Whoever believes that Jesus is the Christ is born of God, and everyone who loves Him who begot also loves him who is begotten of Him (1 John 4:20-5:1).

John makes it clear from these verses that liars are those who deceive others and themselves as to the genuineness of their commitment by saying they love God and yet hate their brother. You might say, "You know, that's a pretty serious accusation," and I would agree with you that it is! But listen to John's reasoning here: "for he who does not love his brother whom he has seen, how can he love God whom he has not seen?" How ridiculous is that? We say we love God and yet we have never seen Him. John made it clear in 1 John 4:12 that no man has seen God at any time. We love Him, yet we don't see Him. So how can we say we love God whom we have never seen, and hate our brother whom we can see? What is the logic here? How can we love God who is invisible when we cannot even love our brother who is visible? John is saying this logic is absurd. I. Howard Marshall says, "A person may deceive other men by declaring that he loves God; but since God cannot be seen, there is no direct way of telling whether he truly loves God. Even as he goes through the outward motions of devotion to God, prayer, attendance of worship, and so on, it may still be all empty show. But a person cannot so easily deceive others regarding his love for his fellow Christians; since they can be seen, the person's relation with them is also visible."[3] A genuine faith in Christ will manifest itself in a love for God which shows itself in loving others. Last, but not least, is the final test in 1 John, which is found in the final verse of this little epistle.

20. The test of keeping ourselves from idols.

> Little children, keep yourselves from idols. Amen (1 John 5:21).

Again we note the tenderness in John's words—*little children*, which means little teknion, little born ones of God. John uses this term of endearment one more time before he ends with his final words to them, *keep yourselves from idols*. The word *keep* means watch, be on guard, regarding idols. What is an idol? An idol is an image, a heathen god, a form, or an appearance—anything or anyone that takes the place of God. An idol is anything that keeps you from making a full commitment to Christ. By the way, this is a command, and it is given in a firm tone as represented by the aorist tense. Now the question comes to mind, "What idols is John talking about? Is he talking about literal idols?" That is a possible interpretation. But there is also another idea and that is that an idol can be anything that replaces God.

Some possible idols of our heart are pleasure, career, success, a goal, a desire, business, wealth, fame, a fine house, and material possessions like furniture, cars, boats,

---

[3] I. Howard Marshall. *The New International Commentary on the New Testament: The Epistles of John* (Grand Rapids, MI: Wm. B. Eerdmans Publishing Company, 1994) p. 225.

and jewelry. Perhaps other idols are friendships, family relationships, self-love, pride, entertainment or sports. In fact, in her book, *The Excellent Wife*, Martha Peace quotes Lou Priolo, who says, "An idol can be anything. It may even be a good thing. But if we want it so badly that we sin if we don't get it or sin to attain it, then we are worshiping an idol rather than Christ."[4] Each of us is worshiping something or someone every waking moment of every day. She also quotes Stuart Scott, who says that we worship what we "serve, speak about, sacrifice for, seek after, and spend time and money on."[5] Some common idols include: good health, physical appearance, having a Christian marriage, being treated fairly, having a hurt-free and pain-free life, and worldly pleasures such as drugs, alcohol, and sex. An idol could be a child or children, another person, material things, money, success, others' approval, being in control, have your needs met, sleep, work, television, reading, food, shopping, sports, exercise, recreation, hobbies, or ministry as an escape.

You might say, "Well, how can I know if my heart is centered on Christ or if I am an idolater?" Some good questions to ask yourself when determining whether or not you are committing idolatry are:

1. What is on your mind most of the time?
2. What do you long for or wish for?
3. What is really important to you?
4. What do you have your heart set on?
5. What or who has your deepest affection?
6. What is your ultimate priority?
7. What is your greatest fear?

---

[4] Martha Peace. *The Excellent Wife* (Bemidji, MN: Focus Publishing, 1995) p. 59.

[5] Ibid.

If you are committing ongoing idolatry it may be an indication that you lack a genuine commitment to Christ.

Let's review briefly all of the 20 tests.

1. *The test of having partnership or fellowship with Christ and the Father*: 1 John 1:3. Do you have fellowship with Him?

2. *The test of joy*: 1 John 1:4. Are you joyful?

3. *The test of confessing our sins*: 1 John 1:9. When is the last time you confessed your sins?

4. *The test of broken pattern of sinning*: 1 John 2:1; 3:4-6; 3:8 9; 5:18. Are you practicing any known sin today?

5. *The test of obedience*: 1 John 2:3-5; 3:22-24; 5:2, 3. Are you obeying God's commandments—all of them?

6. *The test of walking as Christ walked*: 1 John 2:6. Do you walk as Christ walked?

7. *The test of loving the brethren*: 1 John 2:9-11; 3:10-18; 3:23; 4:7-12; 4:20-5:2. Do you love all the brethren?

8. *The test of overcoming the wicked one*: 1 John 2:13, 14; 5:4, 18. Does Satan have any rule in your heart today?

9. *The test of not loving the world*: 1 John 2:15-17; 4:4, 5. Are there any forms of worldliness in your life?

10. *The test of persevering to the end*: 1 John 2:19, 24. Is your life as zealous for the Lord today as last year?

11. *The test of the indwelling Holy Spirit*: 1 John 2:20, 27; 3:24; 4:13. Do you sense the Spirit's leading, convicting, empowering in your life?

12. *The test of belief*: 1 John 2:23; 3:23; 4:2, 15; 5:1, 2, 5,10,13,20. Do you really believe that Jesus is the Christ?

13. *The test of abiding in Him*: 1 John 2:27, 28; 4:16. Are you abiding—remaining—in the Father?

14. *The test of holy living*: 1 John 2:29; 3:3, 7. Are you striving to be perfect as He is perfect?

15. *The test of hatred from the world*: 1 John 3:13. When is the last time you received persecution from the world for your stand for Christ?

16. *The test of answered prayer*: 1 John 3:22; 5:14, 15. When is the last time God answered your prayer?

17. *The test of overcoming false teachers*: 1 John 4:4. Can you discern a false teacher?

18. *The test of no fear in judgment*: 1 John 2:28; 4:17, 18. Are you fearful of the rapture and the judgment to come?

19. *The test of loving God*: 1 John 4:19-5:1. Do you love God? Does it show itself in your actions and by your love to others?

20. *The test of keeping ourselves from idols*: 1 John 5:21. Do you have any idols in your life?

In this uncertain age in which we live, there are numerous things that will remain uncertain and unstable and unknown. But for children of the King, there is one thing that you can know for certain: that you have eternal life. Do you have eternal life? If you do not, why not make that commitment to His Lordship today?

About the Author

Susan Heck and her husband Doug have been married for 37 years. She has been involved in Women's Ministries for about 28 years. This included teaching Bible Studies, counseling, and leading Ladies with the Master women's ministry at Grace Community Church in Tulsa, Oklahoma (www.gccoftulsa.net).

Susan is a certified counselor with the National Association of Nouthetic Counselors (www.nanc.org). She is the author of the Master" Bible Study series for women.

Susan's teaching ministry is an outgrowth of her memorization work on the Bible. She has personally memorized 23 books of the New Testament word-for-word: The Gospel of Matthew, The Gospel of John, Romans, Second Corinthians, Galatians, Ephesians, Philippians, Colossians, First and Second Thessalonians, First and Second Timothy, Titus, Philemon, Hebrews, James, First and Second Peter, First, Second, and Third John, Jude, Revelation, one book of the Old Testament (Jonah), and several other portions of Scripture.

Susan and Doug have two grown children and seven grandchildren. Both children and their spouses are in full-time ministry. Because of the enthusiasm of ladies who have attended Susan's Bible studies, she has been invited to speak to a number of ladies groups both nationally and internationally (www.withthemaster.org).

Susan Heck Resources
Available at www.focuspublishing.com

With the Master on Our Knees
A Ladies' Bible Study on Prayer
With the Master in Fullness of Joy
A Ladies' Bible Study on Prayer

Booklets:
Putting off Life-Dominating Sins
A Call to Discipleship
A Call to Scripture Memory
20 Tests for God's Little Children

With the Master in the School of Tested Faith
A Ladies' Bible Study on the Book of James
Available from www.amazon.com